# PLAGUE

## A Perpetual Struggle in the Lives of Black People

Peter S. Oduwole

authorHOUSE®

*AuthorHouse™*
*1663 Liberty Drive*
*Bloomington, IN 47403*
*www.authorhouse.com*
*Phone: 1-800-839-8640*

*First published by AuthorHouse  6/23/2009*

*ISBN: 978-1-4389-7818-5 (e)*
*ISBN: 978-1-4389-7823-9 (sc)*

*Printed in the United States of America*
*Bloomington, Indiana*

*This book is printed on acid-free paper.*

This book is dedicated to my late sister Patience Oduwole.

# PREFACE

Understanding just how we arrived at this junction in history is very crucial to our salvation from this generational battle. This battle started centuries ago in the year 1441. Portuguese ships first arriving off the Guinea coast in Africa, kidnapped two African males. Antam Goncalve of Portugal took home a kidnapped Berber and his servant as gifts for a Portuguese Prince. Years later, Portuguese raiders kidnapped several Africans and took them away to Portugal as workers and servants. In 1472 Portuguese merchant Ruy do Siqueira formally began the Atlantic Slave Trade.

Upon their arrival in Africa, the Portuguese became extremely amazed at the governmental structure of the African people. There was a national effort to establish a systematic order in the many villages. There was a role for every man, woman, and child in generating productivity for the community where they lived. Farming, hunting, child rearing, midwives, public order, and even means of spiritual worship were carried out with great precision and order. The Portuguese also became familiar with the established empires, and their hegemony control. The Portuguese themselves were an empire, and they were familiar with their treatment of their colonized nations.

The Portuguese became very astounding at how trusting the African people were. The hospitality of the African people was very pleasurable. The Portuguese were free to venture around towns and villages unguarded. They were even invited to dine with towns leaders. The trust worthiness of the Africans became one of their tickets to the new world.

Africans and African Americans have a confound treatment of their guests. There are stories in many African American homes, where families would eat dinner after the local church minister has eaten. Most African American males will welcome a person of another race to a game of basketball or any other form of entertainment in an African American community. African Americans running for public offices work harder to gain votes from other races. Non African Americans work less hard to acquire votes in African American communities. We even sometimes find it harder to win elections against non African Americans in our own community.

We sometimes believe that non-African Americans can do a better job than we can. A very famous celebrity of whom I have great admiration and a great respect for once became very proud, when he realized that his airplane was being piloted by black African pilots. He then became cautious, when there was a little turbulence, and he jokingly asked for the white pilots. He is one of my mentors.

So why do we trust everyone else but ourselves? And why did the Africans with all of their kingdoms, established villages, towns and civilization not stop the carnage of their people into slavery? The following reasons existed. Trustworthiness, the breakdown of their family and senseless wars.

Today we called it black on black crimes or black on black violence. Unlike slavery in Africa, slavery in the Americas was based on race. The Africans had yet to develop racial solidarity among themselves. Slavery took a harsher form when it came to the Americas. In the Americas the slaves became known as CHATTEL----which means personal property of their masters. In Spain, slavery was conducted with what was called ASIENTO (contract). Slavery became easily available to the west due to continued warfare among tribes and kingdoms. This was the beginning of black on black violence. The by-product of these wars in Africa became young black men kidnapped, and sent away into slavery in a far away land. When African kingdoms and States expanded, conflicts between tribes increased and civil unrest escalated.

When more drugs are poured into African American neighborhoods, black on black violence increases, senseless crimes against each other become on the rise. The European traders provided warring tribes with firearms and instigated the chaos, by insinuating both tribes receiving more goods and trades than the other.

Unlike what western history has reported, African women were never sold into slavery. Whether by war, or by difference in dialect or tribe, the African women were responsible for agricultural labor. They were withheld from the Atlantic slave trade by the different kingdoms. Many kingdoms fought to rescue their women from being sent across the Atlantic. This act was still practiced by slaves born in America. Many husbands went back into slavery trying to rescue their wives from their masters.

Blackness is a gift from God. Our smiles, features and complexion have all given us reason to feel pride and indulge self dignity, not only for ourselves, but for every other race. Emotions and opinions are all natural phenomenon of life. When reading this book, try to establish an honest reflection of yourself and our community.

This book is not a condemnation of black people. It is a revelation of hidden obstacles that have threatened and kept us in bondage for centuries. Our history is world history. The Greeks and the Romans have African arts and customs incorporated into their society. Many great nations have parts of Africa within their souls. This is the time for us to face our weaknesses in pursuit of peace and goodwill for all of mankind. This is a call for us to revisit our strength which is family unity. In doing so, we must also embrace all races, because together, our battle will be won much sooner than later. The disunity of the black family has always been the cause of their demise.

# CONTENTS

# CHAPTER 1: THE BEGINNING

Early Egyptians did not view themselves as African or as black people. Arab adventurers called black Africans, Bilad es Sudan, which means, land of the black people. Not surprisingly, modern Egyptians also don't see themselves as Africans. Moroccans , Libyans, Sudanese, Somalis etc would first tell you that they are either Arab or Muslim rather than acknowledging any identity close to Africa. Astonishingly, a growing number of African Americans are somehow avoiding their connections to Africa also. African nations are also sharing this disclaimer of their culture. Black African nations view Arab African nations also as foreigners. So this identity desolation shared by them all, has lead to the infiltration of colonial rule, slavery, poverty, self-doubt and many other pains that have plagued black people for many years.

Throughout this book, we will come across many known facts that have been dwelling in the black community for years, yet, those facts have been kept silent by many. We tend to become angry and denying when one of us make a plead for an end to the self destructive behavior that have plagued us for generations. Black African nations recognized Arab African nations as Africans only for historical or geographical pride. An invasion against a black African nation such as Liberia, Ghana or Sierra Leone is seen by Arab African nations simply as an invasion of one country against another country. The same belief is held by black African nations. However, any invasion against an Arab African nation would be seen by all Arabs as an invasion against them. They would condemn such an invasion and progressively rise up to the country's defense.

We are slowly beginning to experience the origins of disunity among blacks spreading throughout Africa and into the United States. The disunity started first with Africans and then passed on to African Americans. An aggressive act against an African American by a non African American unites all African Americans against the aggressor. An aggressive act by one African American against another is vaguely acknowledged with marches and chants. Poverty, unequal shares of wealth, and social discrimination by powerful leaders are to blame for black on black aggression. Emotions are a very powerful phenomenon within the African American community.

Emotions are even greater within the continent of Africa. Black people are moved by many great causes. However, our emotions create an unraveling push towards our goals in life. Our expressions and interpretations have been defined by colonial power as aggression. An African American male speaking against social injustice is viewed as angry and aggressive. Any other ethnic male speaking against social injustice would only be seen as a political individual.

So how do we then redirect our emotions towards eradicating plagues which have destroyed us for centuries? When there are dissentions among African nations, violence, degradations of human lives, and when the same is practiced by African Americans, how do we stop these plagues? When will black Africans recognize Arab Africans as a black African with a lighter skin tone? And when will Arab Africans recognized black Africans as one of them with a darker tone? When will African Americans truly take a mirror approach towards their internal conflicts which have plagued them for so long? How do African Americans and Africans in Africa begin to finally bring their conflicts to rest? In order to begin this journey, we must first recognize our faults, our weaknesses, and our ongoing problems that are affecting us. We must also recognize all of our strengths.

This is our story-------black America's perception of Africa has been a natural historical set back for centuries. Since slavery, we have always viewed black Africans as uncivilized, inhumane, barbaric, illiterate and stupid. Even educated blacks who are expected to have obtained in depth knowledge of our history, sometimes project dissimulated feelings toward Africans. During slavery newly arrived slaves were laughed at by American born slaves, and even slaves who had assimilated into the American culture rebuked the newly arrived slaves.

The movie "Roots" shared some spot light on this behavior. There were scenes in the movie where slaves born in America projected a self-entitlement attitude toward newly arrived slaves. An attitude that stated we were here first, so we have paid our dues, pay yours. There was a scene in the movie Amistad, where kidnapped slaves where been paraded through the streets. American born slaves laughed and even disassociated themselves from those slaves. Today in modern America, many black Americans believe Africans living in the U.S. receive greater respect and assistance from white America than African Americans.

There is a widespread belief held by many African Americans. The belief is that African students receive free college education in the U.S. Many also believe Africans along with other foreigners are allowed to work without paying taxes for five years. These views were also shared by a doctor on a very popular radio show. Some African Americans are even questioning their African roots. Some are debating being called an African American. Many have claimed to be everything from Indian, German, Irish, and British. And the popular reason for those claims is that the slave masters had children with the slaves and we were all mixed. Ironically, many will assume African heritage when there is a personal glorification to be obtained or when they are faced with any form of racial injustice.

Sometimes pride and ownership are recognized in life when there is a pay off to be gained. Just like the Arab Africans and the black Africans, many African Americans have joined the culture of heritage disassociation unless there is something to be gained.

The continued decline of social and economic empowerment in black society clearly defines the strength of ignorance, denial and civil misunderstanding within our communities. The wealth of Africa is without a doubt a symbol of it's economic might. This fact has been widely known for centuries. The world is much aware of the vast availabilities of natural resources and countless dependable exports that Africa has. These resources are still being provided to the world. Nevertheless, Africa is yet the poorest of the seven continents. Africa like black America has been facing civil disregard, easy persuasions, gross manipulations and self denial throughout it's existence.

In Africa, rural conflicts, tribal wars, senseless cultural battles and derelict leaders have all played many roles into the sad story of slavery. Strong racial, ethnic, and countless stereotypes have been in rule within the African American community for years. Light skinned blacks have been against dark skinned blacks, foreign born blacks have been against blacks born in America and southern blacks have been against northern blacks.

(The movie made about the singing group, The Temptations, showed just how trust was established between the Temps from the south versus the Temps from the north. Although they were all very talented African

American young men, two of them felt the need to trust the other based on geographic origin. So called proper speaking blacks have been frowned on by so called bad grammar speaking blacks. Suburban blacks have also been frowned on by urban blacks. And even blacks who portray professional attributes at work or at social gatherings are also scorned and accused of trying to act white.

# CHAPTER 2:
# OUR PERCEPTIONS

During the early sixties and late seventies, our views of each other were very astounding. Dark skinned blacks had a different view of their light skinned brothers and sisters. Prejudice was very common and acknowledged when it came to skin complexion in the black community.

Many dark skinned black men viewed their light skinned brothers as arrogant, egotistical, self entitled with a pretty boy mentality, untrustworthy and not a true representative of blackness. Similar beliefs were held by light skinned black men against their dark skinned brothers. When grouped with dark skinned black men, some light skinned brothers portrayed a leadership role mentality.

Surprisingly, dark skinned black women shared very similar beliefs about their light skinned sisters. Light skinned sisters were perceived as self entitled, lazy and conceited with a pretty girl mentality. Those same beliefs were held by light skinned sisters toward their dark skinned sisters. Ironically, dark skinned black women insidiously viewed light skinned sisters as beautiful. But when asked in person, they sustained a black is beautiful attitude. There was always conversation held among dark skinned sisters concerning pretty hair and pretty skin features of light skinned women. Many dark skinned sister became very elated when their kids appeared to have pretty hair or a light skin tone. Although they were very reluctant to admit it, many dark skinned black women said they would like to have light skinned kids with pretty hair and features.

Back then some dark skinned black women saw their light skin sisters as male magnets. Many believed that the light skinned sisters drew black men attention when they were out on social events. Many of these confusing beliefs were also held by dark Africans toward light skinned Africans. However, when it came to social events, dark skinned brothers didn't discriminate. They socialized with any brother who could hold himself up. Skin color didn't matter as long as the brother held himself together. Yet, some dark skinned black men cautiously viewed their light skinned brothers untrustworthy when it came to women.

This form of pervasive ignorance and degradation that was shared by many within our continent and within the African American community, have greatly limited social advancements, economic empowerment, and individual responsibility. Misunderstandings among ourselves have perpetuated senseless mistrust, violence and economic ruins in Africa and in the U.S. There is the argument that slavery was enabled by the African leaders. According to some, Africans sold their brothers, sisters and kinfolks to the western world. This argument is undeniable, however there are few truth to it, and it has been far stretched in history. Nevertheless, the real story is at a distance from the history books. Slavery was practiced by just about every civilization throughout history. However, The story of African slavery is told under a different umbrella.

African slaves were mainly used to cultivate land, harvest farms, build villages, and most significantly, go to war against other invading tribes. Many slaves would gradually become set free either for their contributions toward the village or as a gesture of goodwill by the local chief. Many slaves married into tribes that held them captive, bore children and became very patriotic to the regimen of their new homes. The inclement practice of slavery in the Americas was a far cry from the way and manner in which slavery was practiced in Africa.

The dominance of western persuasions over the Africans have always been questioned by scholars. There have always been a variation of persuasion based on tribes, locations, dialects and religion. Slavery according to today's definition was introduced by Muslim travelers into western Africa. Yet, the Muslims themselves didn't practice slavery with such brutality and prejudicial mindset as we have known it to have been practiced in the west. The Muslims used captured slaves as concubines, servants and gifts to their leaders. The Muslims were more concerned with spreading the doctrine of Islam to the Africans than they were about capturing African slaves.

Since the beginning of modern civilization, there have been several instituted excuses made by sponsors and co-sponsors of slavery. There have been many failed attempts made trying to rewrite one of the darkened page of world history. We need to understand why slavery lasted for so long. What was the hidden force that blinded the Africans from seeing such evil that was brought upon their land? And how can we learn from the mistakes made by the Africans? In order for us to understand why, we must travel back to black America.

Black on black crimes have been a generational experienced in just about every black community. Social and religious ignorance, and the loss of kinship have all contributed toward the longevity of our generational demise. The prevalence of violence and social chaos have kept us very preoccupied and non observant toward outside influences on our demise.

The bible tells us of the story of the tower of Babel. God created confusion and miscommunication among the people in order to stop them from building the tower. The Israelites won many battles due to chaos among their enemies. When there is dissension in a marriage the door is opened to the devil's plan. When there are problems in a community intruders are always welcome in.

The Roman Empire fell not from outside invaders, but due to internal conflicts. The Africans didn't realize this trend, and African Americans seem to follow the same. Little attention is paid toward the strength of a family today in the African American community. We have lost the power and protection of a united family. We have truly forgotten the reasons why families were separated during slavery. The strength of any victory in a community is sustained by the inclusiveness and recognition of family unity.

Negative views held by many African Americans toward Africa have salvaged this long lasting impudent climate of social injustice toward black people as a whole. The level of ignorance can not even begin to unravel among us. Many African Americans believe that Africa is a country. When asked if Africa could be a vacation destination, many African Americans frown on taking such a trip. The diseases of ignorance, hypocrisy, and self denial have kept us at a devalued state in today's global changes. The world is still in a deniable state when faced with the magnitude and the impact that the slave trade has left on it. Although moral and religious values are recognized when the act of slavery is being discussed, they have yet to be acted upon. The story of Africa should be a global reminder to those who seek to eradicate any resemblance of hate and genocidal threat to mankind.

# CHAPTER 3:
## OUR IGNORANCE

The survival of Africa is also the survival of African American pride and dignity to themselves and to their history. We have become a market to the business of hypocrisy and self cynicism. Questions of pride and self worth are indulged by us as long as we are not questioning ourselves. We have become less patronizing to ourselves and our culture than we are to other cultures. African names are laughed at and ridiculed by us more than any other ethnic names.

We seem to accurately pronounce Hispanic, European, Indian, and even Asian names well without any demeaning, or verbal denouncements. Effective communication leads to cultural understanding. The idea is to create self-awareness and a verbal communicative attitude towards one another with regard to respect and pride.

We now have the will, the way, the power, and the voices to exercise a strength that we had all along. Yet, we refute our capabilities in exercising our responsibilities. We have to truly recognize our strengths and our weakness in order for us to truly move into our long awaited rightful place in history. The global coronation is yet to be held. Celebrating unity, peace, and global prosperity should be one of our many goals. We need to admonish ourselves in the presence of foolishness and stupidity. Crime and self-instituted ignorance should be eradicated permanently. The glorification and silence to community crimes should be stood up against by everyone of us old and young.

When President Barack Obama ran for the Illinois Senate, his rival was Alan Keys. Mr. Keys became the ambassador for self stupidity, cultural discrimination, and a simple disgrace to himself. He claimed that because President Obama's father wasn't born in America, President Obama should not be called an African American. As foolish as this may sound, there is a consensus dwelling among some in the African American community concerning the identity of Africans living in America. Some African Americans believe that the term black should not be prescribed to a black person living in America who was not born in America. You would many times hear an African American asking if a black person from the Caribbean or other parts of the world is black?

The New York Times National published an article on Sunday, August 29, 2004 concerning the term African American. Abdulaziz Kamus, an Ethiopian born American citizen, said according to the article, "blacks whose ancestors where slaves did not see him as African American." This view is held by many foreign blacks living in America. The article also mentioned very unbelievable remarks made by the black republican challenger for the senate seat, Alan Keys.

As mentioned earlier, Mr. Keyes questioned whether president Obama should claim African American identity. Mr. Keyes told George Stephanopoulos on the ABC program "This Week" "Barack Obama and I have the same race that is, physical characteristics. We are not from the same heritage." He went on to say that, "My ancestors toiled in slavery in this country, my consciousness, who I am as a person, has been shaped by my struggle, deeply emotional and deeply painful, with the reality of that heritage."

Questioning who is entitled to the civil rights benefits is now becoming a talk within the African American community. Former secretary of state Collin Powell, who is also a son of a Jamaican immigrant, has been seen as another undeserving foreign black person by some within the African American community.

The impact of slavery and it's assault and stain is currently ravishing the continent of Africa. Long lasting anguish, pain, despondency and loss have dwelt in villages, towns, families, and individuals since slavery. The movie Roots showed a village still waiting for their lost son to return home even after centuries of captivity. Africa is now embedded with several languages due to slavery. Among the many languages are French, Dutch, Portuguese and English. The strength of family unity practiced by Africans have all but disappeared from the continent since the arrival of colonialism.

Negative views of Africa didn't just begin in the 20th century. These views have been the pillars that up-lifted aggrandizing blacks against newly arrived slaves on the plantation. The sense that many of these blacks incorporated self-abasement countenance is self-pity. Poet Phillis Wheatley was an advocate of white culture. She stressed that black people should adopt white culture. According to history, she lived exclusively among whites before she married. Phillis felt very grateful to have been brought to America. According to her, mercy brought her out of a pagan land. Although she spoke against slavery and the treatment of slave, her views of Africa was very degrading.

Samuel Cornish was one of the first publicist of the Freedom Journal, (the first black newspaper). He was a young Presbyterian minister in 1827. He avidly regarded himself as an American with no ties to Africa. The campaign made by the American Colonization Society to send blacks to Africa where they believed the blacks would be truly free did not work well with Cornish and many others. Cornish and other blacks considered Africa to be a foreign place that was very unhealthy and they had no desire to go there.

A doctor appeared on a very popular morning show. He said when he asked ten (10) African Americans if he came from the past and told them what would happen to them and their ancestors being put into slavery and the  degradation  of the slaves, along with  Jim Crow's segregation, and the many atrocities associated with slavery. If they were standing on line to board a slave ship and they were told these facts would they still board the ship?  He  says stunningly, seven (7) out of ten (10) African American  said they would board the ship and come to America. Our pride, prestige, and disassociation from Africa have been a generational gift handed down from one generation to the other since slavery.

Chaos and family disunity among the African people sustained the longevity of slavery in Africa. Chaos and family disunity among African American have also sustained the black on black violence that we have witnessed over the many years. We had lost our focus a long time ago. While we were fighting among ourselves, an evilness insidiously crept into our villages, our homes, and into our children. We all need to start from within our communities in order to end this curse.

The success of slavery came only due to easy persuasions by European slave merchants. Black people are historically the easiest people that can be persuaded.  Many of us believe that someone else can do a better job than we can. A white pilot is more trusted than a black pilot. White neighborhoods, white professors, white doctors, and even white friends somehow portray success according to many of us.

# CHAPTER 4:
# PRAISE AND WORSHIP

W hy do we discredit ourselves, mistrust ourselves, and even become malevolent against
one another? The black church has been a major contributor to some of our perversity. It has been
a magnificent breeding ground for powerless thinkers,
spiritual miscarriages and in many instances the mis-
informed. Although the church owed credit to many
ladders that we have climbed, it still is a strong proxy
force in the black community.

The black church has always been a platform for
unity, strength, and spiritual guidance. Yet, it holds
some responsibilities towards our pitfalls in society.
With many great successes, there have also been many
great failures. Great leaders such as Dr. King, Absalom
Jones and countless others have paved the way for
spiritual strength, self-respect, and self-pride. Those efforts and works by our past leaders can be compared to

none. We now stand today with a calamity of problems within some black churches. With their great influences on the black community, some black pastors have been using the pulpit as a breeding ground to attain personal success and mismanaged goals. We have heard many stories of church pastors sorrows and failures. However, we do not have any clue as to how imminent this plaque is upon the black community.

The black church was the only institution in America to which the slaves could go for self-dignity and spiritual direction. Slaves coming from Africa did not have to be forced or strongly convinced to become Christians. The functions of the Christian church were very much replicas of the Africans tribal customs back home in Africa. The dances, singing, speaking in tongues, and even the baptism were all symbolic of how they used to celebrate back in Africa. They had a spiritual leader back in the village. In America, there was the priest or pastor. They sang and danced during times of tribal celebration in Africa . In the church, there was singing and dancing among the saints. There were cultural practices that involved going to the river and performing ritual acts in accordance to African customs. Being baptized in water appeared similar to those ritual acts.

So when the slaves were introduced to Christianity in America, they basically saw many similarities to their African customs. And there we have the beginning of control and insidious mind directions of a nation of people who will in return, reciprocate the same to one another.

So with the church having total influence over the African slaves, the cycle of betrayal began very early. Pastors and ministers told the congregations to obey their masters because it was the right thing to do as a Christian. The slaves saw nothing wrong with that order since they already obeyed their voodoo priests back in Africa. Many black families saw the need to belong to a church because of their ancestral influences. So the seed of persuasion was established from a very early stage in the lives of black people by the church.

Today some black preachers have rewritten the scriptures under the umbrella of salvation, financial growth and spiritual blessings. Some of the same messages were preached to the slaves by their masters with biblical interjections. In every urban city in America we find over a hundred or more black churches. There are churches on streets, avenues and some private homes. However, the most crimes committed in America are committed in those areas with the many churches standing near-by. With the many outreach programs administered by some of those churches, one would expect urban crimes to depreciate. It now seems like those churches are preaching to the choir. Sadly, many of those churches are becoming victims to urban crimes as well.

Churches are being broken into for aluminum steel, doors and windows have been taken off their hinges. Despite some of the many perils of the black church, there are also many great and unprecedented achievements made by a growing number of vision driven leaders. These churches have escaped the old ways of functioning, such as perpetuated building funds, little progress in their local communities and negative labels that have been attached to them. Here in our local community there are several churches that have succeeded in community progress. These churches have created back to school programs, child care services, finance and health care seminars, job fairs and community involvement.

Americans have an established loyalty when it comes to the church. Most Americans hold a special bond to their religious principles and values regardless of unknown circumstances. We saw how pivotal a role religion played in the (2000) presidential election. Many blacks ignored their depreciating economic status, rising health cost and crime and voted for the republican party based only on religious principles.

Although the republican party has a history of doing nothing for the African American community, it was successful in acquiring a majority vote based on fear and religion. The hypocrisy of religion is still prevalent within our culture. It's strength has much power and influence on most Americans and a greater influence on the black community.

Families have been disunited due to religious conflicts. Marriages have been destroyed due to religious battles. World history has in its archives destruction caused by religious warfare. Religious giants and leaders are aware of the influence they can have on world policies. As mentioned earlier, the African slaves were coerced through religion. The Ku Klux Klan based many of it's principles and values on religious orders.

The perennial efforts of the church are very strong and have survived mainly, because church leaders have a united effort to maintain their status individually and to reap the many benefits that the church has to offer. The social complexity of church leaders and their values have been a phenomenon constructed with brilliance. During slavery the priests would stand in front of the slave ship and bless the slaves before they make the journey to America. Many church leaders today are known for sinful deeds done against the church and the community. However many seem to come out still retaining their titles and staff.

Within the African American community, most if not all of the church pastors live miles away from their church. A growing number of their members also live several miles away from their church also. Coming to church on a Sunday is an event. The early morning preparations which consist of clothes, hats, and shoe selections are all part of this grand event. The payoff to this grand event for some is the offering march or altar call which enables them to display their church attire.

When the head of the black Baptist alliance was caught with embezzlement and adultery, and after he had done jail time for his criminal act, he assumed his duty as before and no one was expected to questioned him. We all knew him as the head of world com. Renown for his religious antics, his involvement in the high tech world. God's name was mentioned during speeches and interviews. He presided over one of the largest frauds in US history. Many lost their retirement and investments due to his fraud. While facing federal charges and under indictment in Oklahoma, he tearfully told his congregation that he hopes this doesn't jeopardize his witness for Jesus Christ.

# CHAPTER 5: A NEW TREND /FALSE BELIEFS

Church leader misconduct is easily forgiven by the congregation with words such as it is the work of the devil or the devil is busy. As simple as these excuses may sound they have had profound results on many black congregations. Many of these churches are under denominational rule. So, many of their members have a certain loyalty to their church based on denomination. There are others who claim family longevity.

On any given Sunday, there is a rainfall of messages from church pulpits warning members against leaving their church or having ill feelings toward church improprieties. Terms such as church hopping are frequently used to discourage members from visiting other churches. Unfortunately, the mentality of see no evil, hear no evil and say no evil of your church have been brought into many black neighborhoods. Culprits to senseless crimes in our neighborhoods are not reported nor spoken of leaving anarchy and social ruins to rule our streets and homes. Grandparents who sat in the back of buses yesterday so that we can today sit in the front, today can no longer walk their streets and neighborhoods in fear of youth crimes and violence.

Material adorations and aspirations have become prevalent in many black churches today. Pastor's anniversary is an occasion geared toward raising money for the pastor in addition to his salary. First lady's night and many other known farces that have become accepted have caused many sleepless nights for many mothers and single mothers in the church. Women in the church have become prime targets for religious manipulation.

The African American women are a major acquisition in the black church. Black women make up 95% of most African American church in America. Their commitments and devotions are second to none when it comes to church affairs. Church pastors and leaders are aware of these women strong loyalties to the church. When we identify our problems and admit to our faults, we begin a process of healing and resurrecting ourselves to a new direction. As black people we just cannot sit down anymore and allow past excuses, denial, and false pretenses to continuously divide us.

We have to become very proactive toward undutiful behaviors and become vocal in denouncing rambunctious acts that have been accepted in the past. We cannot allow our families and friends to fall apart anymore. We should possess positive attributes and become more ambition driven in our communities. We should demand that our women and young girls exercise class and pride for themselves. And our men and young boys a much higher demand of self respect, family and community honor.

We have condoned many negative stereotypes for years in our homes and community. Town hall meetings and marches have exposed those stereotypes but have not eradicated them. A common belief held in the black community is that black children are better behaved in public than white children are. Jokes and stories have been told by our comedians describing how a black mother's dirty look in public brings her disgruntled child's anguish to a halt. A white mother on the other hand will continuously beg and plead with her child to stop misbehaving in public.

The logic behind this belief is to indicate the disciplinary authority that we have over our children. Sometimes a single look deters our kids from misbehaving. If this belief stands to be true then why are many of our young men involved in drugs and violence? Why all of a sudden are our beautiful young princesses exercising behaviors indignity to themselves. Our mitigated actions over the years have lead us into the current abyss we are now facing. Wrong decisions and self indulgences have created a generation of unguarded young people headed to a precluded future. Just like the preacher says, "don't just sit there, do something".

We have sat down for too long. It is time for all of us to do something.

Today there is a new trend spreading in the black community. What is this trend? Being called to preach the word of God and pastoring your own church. Many of our young black men are proclaiming to have been called to preach the word of God. Although many of them are not spiritually mature, they believe they have what it takes to pastor a congregation.

There were several young ministers right after the Great Awakening. Absalom Jones, Richard Allen, Sojourner Truth, Jupiter Hammon, Daniel Coker of Baltimore, John Chavis and other young men and women became involved in the church at very young ages. They sought spiritual and self-healing duties to God and to their people while facing some of the most denigrating deeds done to mankind. They were not seeking fortune or fame as many do today and their services did not depict a trend.

Too many of our young black men have taken on these religious trends and they have created self-prescribed titles for themselves. Among the many titles that they call themselves are reverend, bishop, pastor and spiritual counselor. Some have even claimed themselves to be honorary doctors.

Many of these young black men acquire store front churches in black neighborhoods. They rent existing sanctuaries to support their practice of playing church. In our community a church is a church regardless of it's physical structure. There is now a growing competition among these young black preachers. On any given Sunday, there is a trial sermon to be heard by another young preacher who claimed to have been called to the ministry. Spiritual maturity, wisdom and true biblical understanding are some of the tools missing by these young preachers. Prerequisites to the ministry are the trial sermon, a support staff of other young black preachers and a first lady.

Other unspoken requirements to being a preacher in the black church today are your attire, your language, and the type of car that you drive. Sounding very theological and prophetic among your peers is also a very important requirement for many of our young black preachers. And when you greet people you must start by saying praise the Lord. When you do some of those things, you have begun to establish your divine presence among men.

When a local church pastor and three of the church trustees got a second mortgage on the already paid for church, they claimed the church needed repairs and maintenances. They did not fulfill their claim and the church was left with a $200,000 debt. A judgment of foreclosure was issued against the church by the bank. All of these things occurred without the knowledge of the general members of the church. When the members were informed by the media, the church was already in the process of being auctioned within a couple of days. The pastor along with the three trustees went to a local friend for financial help. The deed and ownership of the church now belonged to the friend.

# Chapter 6: Excuses and False Dreams

There is a standing belief within the black community that slavery in America helped to create disunity among black people. This belief led many blacks to associate violence, crime and individual irresponsibility to slavery. There is a generational scar that was left on us from slavery. But we have to remove those scars ourselves. We have been called many names since slavery, and we have answered to all of those names. Our name calling began with names such as blacks, negro, colored people, black American and currently African American.

We have always accepted many of those names. If you ask any black person in the United States or Africa what are some of the problems that are destroying black people? The very first answer you will receive will be that there is disunity among black people. Ironically, we all know our problems, and we also know the answers to those problems. Unfortunately, we have been looking everywhere else to find those answers but at home. Repetitious denials have engulfed our minds. When we do not understand ourselves and our culture we leave ourselves in an atmosphere of dissipation and despondency.

After school programs such as football and basketball seem to be a bargaining tool used to sway our youths away from crime and other illegal activities. Sports activities have been a strong endorsement by many black parents. Science and leadership programs along with civil service, and other beneficial community programs that will establish a strong foundation toward financial growth and individual maturity should be strongly enforced. Although a few of these programs already exist, our community is not aggressively utilizing them.

History tells us that our forefathers and mothers did not have after school programs growing up. Many of them did farm work, and some even quit school in order to help with the welfare of their family. Despite the atmosphere of segregation and other forms of degradation they persevered and owned an insolent attitude toward greatness and freedom. Some of our current leaders either lived through or were second hand witnesses to those forms of deprivation. Hundreds of unknown African American leaders have paved the way for us with their blood, sweat and tears. Some of those leaders grew up without community centers, or the technological availabilities that we have today. The luxury of owning a television in many black homes was a rarity. They strived with dignity and pride in pursuit of freedom and equality for themselves and their fellowman.

Today's blessings were yesterday's dreams held by our parents. Good jobs, health care, home ownership, educational opportunities, freedom to travel, to vote and the opportunity of having an African American representative in our government were dreams held by our forefathers. Today, many of us are taking those dreams for granted. A sense of ambiguity is floating in the air.

Materialism and social entertainment are pursued by many of our youth. As I mentioned earlier, the youth of today possess material things that were never heard of by their parents and older grandparents. If we realize how powerful and strong we can be if we put away foolish behaviors and strive to attain positive goals for ourselves and our country, the results will become astounding. The strength of the bus boycott in the south created an awareness to some of our strength and capabilities. We are at an unprecedented state in our lives. We now have privileges that are still dreamed of by third world countries.

The garnish of privileges and opportunities wasted by our youth and a total denigration of their lives overshadow the progress that was made by our forefathers. A hegemony of sexual and civil disobedience have become rampant among the youth. An entire race is held hostage and is facing a chaotic realm of destruction and anarchy. Our elders are becoming more and more afraid of the youth. Our young black girls have evolved into something of the unknown. Self-respect and pride no longer exist. The act of dating has no significance to our young girls. A hook up is a behavior that is widely accepted by our youth.

Today a young girl meets a guy, has sex with him and moves on. When she sees him with another girl the next day there is no regret.

Many of our children did not even know who James Brown was when he died. A young African American male asked me if the late Coretta Scott King was the wife of Don King during her funeral broadcast on television. Knowledge of our roots and the history of our people is slowly evaporating into thin air. Even in the arts and entertainment arena, legends such as Miles Davis, Mahalia Jackson, George Duke, Duke Ellington, Dizzy Gillespie, are unknown to our youth. This is not a do not blame the white man book.

This is a mirror book. We should now look at ourselves and our demises. We must begin to finally take action against those that are destroying our communities, our values and our strengths. We must take imminent steps toward finding solutions to eradicate this wrath of destruction and disunity that have been a thorn in all of our sides for many years.

When the great philosopher Socrates was executed, the reason for his execution according to the Greek law was for the corrupting of the youth. We have to start firmly with our young boys and girls. Order and punishment with regard to rehabilitation should be enforced. We know there are many fingers to be pointed.

Let us first look at some executives in the music industry. Music was the original meal ticket out of the ghetto. A hit record would instantly get you out of the ghetto according to some beliefs. Many artists were not held to ethical or moral standards. Infidelities, drugs and promiscuity were the badges of honor of the time.

Exploited careers and loss of individuality were spewing into many communities. Many artists went bankrupt. Others basically lived in the homes of their producers. Tours lasted for months, leaving many broken homes, marriages and communities. And just when it could not get any worse, the sport industry became the new meal ticket out of the ghetto. Every young black man wanted to become a sport superstar. Today, the meal ticket dream is shared between both the music and sport industries. Many of our youth are in pursuit of becoming the next musical superstar or the next multimillion dollar athlete. Ironically, getting out of the ghetto is not a dream anymore. Selling negative images of the ghetto has become a birthright for want to be superstars. Ghetto thug life is the ideal image today.

Having bullet wounds or being arrested and sent to jail for senseless crimes are indicative of being a true thug. Unlimited skin tattoos and skimpy outfits are also a required image. True talent is no longer a requirement.

Today, sexual exploitation of young black women in music videos along with profanities and mayhem have become badges of honor. This mayhem has reached every corner of our society. Kids with academic honors in school have also become involved. Kids from virtuous homes and neighborhoods are committing unspeakable crimes.

# CHAPTER 7:
# SELF DESTRUCTION

Kids with fundamental Christian upbringings have also joined the choir of destruction. Good values and moral standards are scorned and avoided by many of our youths today. Our children have learned to avoid traditional values. An American with Italian descent would claim to be an Italian American. An American of jewish descent calls himself a Jewish American. The same can be said for every other ethnic group with the exception of African Americans. We seem to always questioned and scorn our identity. Some even refuse to admit that they are from the south. Our children have learned from us.

What would happen if President Obama claimed to be a Caucasian and not an African American? The level of disappointment and despair in the African American community would be unprecedented. There will be tears and anger and loss of hopes and dreams for many.

We feel very proud knowing that our president not only carries our heritage but our skin color. He has outstanding academic achievements and his character and attributes speak the language of humility. He embraces his ethnicity and heritage from both of his parents.

President Obama is admired and adored world wide, not for his skin color but, for what he stands for. So the question asked is what do we embrace, and what do we stand for? We must accept that which identifies us as black people. His rising to the ultimate power in our country has only one explanation, GOD! Seeing him on television or hearing his very distinguished voice on the radio brings sudden hope and joy to me and many people. The bible tells us that God tells his people that he will disown those that disown him. Disowning our heritage and ethnicity brings about despair and ambiguity.

There is a major transformation going on in the world. Heritage and cultural recognition have risen bringing forth a global understanding of people of all origins and creed. We must not be left behind. Since becoming President of the United States, President Obama has been linked to several country's DNA. The Africans, the Irish, the middle Eastern, and even Asian countries are all claiming him as a son of their soil. In recognizing this ethnic transformation in the world a wave of resentment should umbrella our communities with regard to accepting who we are.

As a mode of legitimizing popular discontent and with the steady increased of cultural ignorance by our youths, we must put out an outcry for cultural education. We can not allow ignorance and hypocrisy to become polarized into a cultural norm. The break down of our families and communities is the writing on the wall for us to wake up and finally do something. Parents should demand full rights and common sense law allowing them to strongly discipline and chastise their children. The laws should be strongly geared toward children who have personally chosen to indulge in delinquent behaviors. Mandatory drug testing should be enforced in all schools, starting with middle school.

Democracy is infallible and freedom is a blessing. We can not continue to define freedom of speech by applying non-beneficial principles to our daily lives. A juvenile is deterred from making a bad decision if the punishment is great. Options are always weighed before bad behavior is acted upon. During the early 70s and 80s, alcoholic bums and delinquent kids had respect for their elders. Wine and marijuana were put away when an older person was approaching the area. The worst kid on the block still had respect and fear for his elders. Something happened along the way to the modernization of our society. Young men and women should be individually held accountable for choices that they make in life. The excuses of many people have heightened this lawlessness throughout the nation. Why do most foreign born children succeed in America?

Foreign born children succeed due to the strong discipline and forceful values from their parents. A delinquent foreign child in most situations, is the product of the pampering privilege  that we have in our system. According to some experts, spanking your child is monstrous.  Speaking to your child harshly is psychological abuse and time out becomes intellectual abuse.

We have allowed our intelligence to become  manipulated by a false definition of democracy. Profanities in public by the youth, hanging out on streets corners, and plain stupidity are the normally accepted forms of our own interpretation of democracy. Media opinion becomes our logic. Words have become very influential toward our understanding of logic.  Liberal and  conservatives, far left, far right, in the middle, centralist and many other senseless words have become acceptable in our way of thinking.

We have destroyed our strength by insidiously endorsing self-destructive behaviors that are now hard to eliminate. The nightmares of our fathers have become the dreams of their sons.  Why dream of a higher education when you can earn lots of money selling drugs in the streets? What is the fear or shame of going to jail, when you gain credibility from the streets and from your family.  Rights and benefits, privileges, and even opportunities are all available when you go to jail. Recovery and job programs are at your disposal.  Housings and  marriage opportunities are also available in jail. Some democratic rights have become democratic demons in today's society.

Self-entitlement attitude is becoming the norm to almost all races. Everybody feels somebody owes them something in life. Ironically, everyone seems to think the next person is responsible for society's problems. The thought of holding ourselves accountable for our behavior is almost unheard of today. Most people disclaim their role in the dysfunction of today's conflicts. We have ceased to exercise resourceful decision making. Civil Rights pioneers who have labored hard and long for freedom and equality are made scapegoats for society's perils. There is a wave of presumptuous reproach being made against the poor.

Cultural ignorance and cynicism have polarized our communities and our homes. The prosperity of our community is at risk. Rambunctious behaviors are endorsed by many of us. We have relegated our pride and dignity in exchange for rogue attitudes. Our places of worship have lost their respect and fear. People are being shot in churches and thieves no longer have fear or respect for the house of God.

Economic hardship and denied opportunities always seem to take the blame for bad behavior. Community outrage has become selectively applied based on the issue of the day. Grandma and grandpa have vastly become obsolete. We have allowed false caricature to become our identities. Derogatory words are used when we are referring to one another. Bitches, whores, my nigger and hood rats are words that we have commercialized. Our image around the world is very laughable. Every negative stereotype to mankind is either applied to Africa or African Americans.

# CHAPTER 8:
# UNITY

We were told that AIDS and Ebola originated in Africa. Although many of us refuted those claims, we did not fight to abolish such nonsense.

According to many false beliefs, the welfare system was a refuge to many African Americans. We did not fight to abolish this either. Extreme hardliners and political opportunists rode on the bandwagon of welfare reform in order to pursue their hidden agendas.

A welfare state is a state that assumes primary responsibility for the individual and social welfare of its citizens. We all should apply this definition toward our quest for progressive unity and understanding among us. The welfare of our brothers and sisters should be the primary goal for everyone of us.

Social and ethnic threats have always been reasons for waging wars. Both World War I and World War II harbored social and economic reasoning. We can not say much about the Gulf War of the nineties. Property qualifications were insisted upon the poor in order to vote during the early centuries in our nation's history. The measurement of discrimination sometimes have no boundaries. Under the umbrella of unity and values, we can restored the true definition of a community.

When people were denied social and economic opportunities, welfare became their only hope. Many people became emotionally and financially concerned after hearing the false stories about the welfare system. Countless nights were spent on television documentaries concerning the welfare system. Fear and financial panic became a norm throughout the nation.

Today we are seeing that many of those so-called welfare recipients were not only Black or Hispanic, they were poor people. And those who were screaming crucify them, have now lost their homes and jobs due to a long standing economic problem in our country.

The strength of the underground railroad was unity. Black people were very united toward the freedom of everyone. No one person was more important than the other during the slaves plight toward freedom. There were stories of free men going back to rescue their wives and kinfolks out of slavery. Many of those men became recaptured by the slave masters.

The stories of Harriet Tubman, Sojourner Truth, Cinque, Madison Washington, Lewis Tappan, Charles T. Torrey and Thomas Garrett were stories of strength courage and unity.

Lives and freedoms of many were given up for the safety and freedom of others. Under the spirit of unity and Christian principles many whites also made great sacrifices towards the freedom of slaves.

This time we need to march for cultural understanding, civil tranquility and global prosperity. The wealth of this great nation and it's standing for equality, civility, peace and justice for all is in abundance. We are a very blessed nation and a loving people who can achieve greatness if we all work together.

The Civil Rights Movement was strongly supported under the unification of good hearted people. Whites, Jews, Asians and all of mankind supported the struggle. Race was insignificant to the three young men killed in Mississippi who were campaigning for voting rights. The voting rights law was supported and encouraged by many young white men and women. When viewing the march to Washington, there are many images of young white men and women marching for justice, freedom and equality. We know the strength of unity and the weakness of silence.

The independence of many African nations evolved from the desire of revolutionary aspirations and global concerns. The song of unity and cultural understanding has been sung for too long with many unsatisfactory results. In Africa, we have war torn nations, genocidal regime, and rogue leaders who seek after their own good and not the good of their people. And in the United States, we have a blatantly chaotic break down of many of our homes and communities.

Ironically when we were colonized in Africa, we exercised obedience, patience, and some form of social stability. Despite the fight for freedom and pockets of civil uprising, family unity was strongly embedded. When African women wore a single garment to cover up their nakedness, they were never raped or sexually violated by their men. Sons became apprentices to their fathers and daughters were taught how to become ladies by their mothers.

During the early years of Apartheid in South Africa, a tone of unity and civil obedience toward authority and kinfolks was established. Protests against the oppressors seldom resulted to violence. Other African nations only spoke against the system of apartheid but without any zeal.

And when some African nations ventured to stage a freedom fight they were cautioned by the West to abort the suggestion. Surprisingly, blacks in the south carried the same banner of unity and family during times of despair.

When people are either colonized or controlled by proxy, unity and civility rule the day. When the Spaniard became the deliverers of order by the spreading of Christianity and civilization to the world, many other western nations followed in pursuit. People tend to act okay with their kinfolks when there is a watchful eye over them. The occurrence of violence is at a minimum.

Since the end of Apartheid, South Africa has become one of the most dangerous countries in the world.

Very violent crimes including rape and torture seem to be the norm in South Africa. So the question then becomes, why do victims always become villain? When the British left India, the Hindus and the Muslims went to war with each other. When the Russians left Afghanistan, the local tribes went to war against each other.

The British were known as the fathers of industrialization. They invented farm machines, advanced navigational systems, and powerful weapons as the world began to move into an advanced state. Modern technology became the new world aspirations. Many nations raced to achieve some form of invented technology. African nations joined in the race, but with a very huge price to pay. They became financial debtors to powerful western nations. Decades later, Africa has become the highest borrower in the world.

It is believed that it will take more than a century to pay off the debts of Africa. Nevertheless, the Africans can not show anything for its debts owed to western nations. African Americans make up more than half the people with consistent purchasing power. Shoes, clothes and other material possessions have been in huge demand in our community. However, we are not the providers of those goods that are in demand.

# CHAPTER 9:
# WHO ARE WE?

My Christian faith and up bringing have always directed my thoughts and decisions in life. We need to include some spiritual guidance in our daily decisions. We need to ask ourselves why do I think this way? Why am I allowing myself to assume these things? Spiritual wisdom should become a daily sought after gift by us. Jacob would not let go of an angel until he was blessed. We need to continuously seek spiritual wisdom in our lives.

The May 2004 issue of Essence Magazine ran an interview with a certain doctor on the issue of skin color. The doctor quoted her mother telling her not to play in the sun because she would have to get a light skinned husband for the sake of her children. Her mother was afraid of her becoming dark by playing in the sun. She indicated many instances when skin complexion became the focal concern and most importantly, a problem for many blacks. Michael Jackson is not the only black person concerned with skin color. We know that this issue of skin color exists amongst us. However, we become angry whenever one of us expresses a concern.

The disease of complacency have to be eliminated. The so called black values have become laughable. We criticize white parents parenting skills, yet, many of our kids are either in jail or delinquent. We frown on white parents adopting black kids because we think black culture will not be properly taught to the adopted child. However, many black parents know very little about African civilizations or African American history. We have taken on habits and customs of other cultures.

Black people are committing suicides and some have even become serial murderers. Today there are black families being slaughtered by fathers, mothers and children. More and more African Americans are placed on psychiatric medication than ever before. We are continuing to have excuses and blames for every fault of ours. And if we could only imagine what our ancestors went through we would be thankful for what we have today.

A day in the life of most African Americans consist of waking up early for work, getting the kids to school and leaving for work. African American culture or history are seldom mentioned at home. Some may argue that the way of life is African American culture. Although segregated policies were implied in order to eliminate our customs we lightly succumbed to those policies. It was imperative for the slaves, especially the Mandingo slaves, that their customs and culture remained and was practiced in the family.

Today in some African nations attending business functions in African attire indicate a degree of primitive indulgence. Wearing suits and tie at business settings show civility. The blessings and opportunities of the industrial revolution and modern medicines was a gift to Africa but a curse in disguise. Western culture and beliefs have been widely accepted by many third world African nations as a sign of civilization. Many third world nations have denounced some of their customs and culture practice in adopting those of many western countries as a sign of social advancement.

The perception of race, and the many beliefs developed giving meaning to physical visibility and differences, have left a denouncing effect on individual's self-image and on the relationship between many groups of people due to colonialism, and ethnic diversities. There have been too many historical journeys all in the quest to uphold race or ethnicity. We can defeat racism. We can defeat black on black crime and we can defeat the many false perceptions that we have of ourselves and other races.

Speaking English properly is not trying to sound white. We need to eliminate such beliefs among us. Ghetto life styles and mentalities are not part of African American culture. We need to stop projecting that belief. The term ghetto was not invented in Africa or by African Americans.

A ghetto environment is not an African American environment. There is no such thing as speaking ghetto or acting ghetto. When a black person acts unruly he is not acting ghetto. We need to stop associating negative words and behaviors with our race. Our ability and capacity to implement positive ideals in our homes and communities is now.

# CHAPTER 10:
# OUR ROLES AND FAMILY

We have helped ridicule ourselves and our culture for too long.

Africa is not a jungle. If we become ashamed of where we have come from we are definitely going to be ashamed of where we are going. We then become a people with no vision for the future. Many of our children are ashamed of who they are and where they have come from. They have created a self doubting spirit within themselves.

In most relationships it is one individual who is working extra hard to keep balance and strength. Most marriages survive because one spouse refuses to quit. We all have to participate in the fight to re-establish unity among us. This fight does not belong to one person only.

Based upon the African custom and culture, leadership is the driving force behind the prosperity of the African village. It is always one or two individuals within our community who uplift us toward greatness and the visions for our community. It is clearly understandable that we all cannot and will not respond to the same ideas and visions of a leader. However, we must strive to understand the strength of unity and the force of self-discrimination that has divided us. It was a united strength that kept us afloat during the great middle passage. With uplifting spirits and blessings from above, we all have stood up against the perils of hate and we have survived.

The burdens of self-hate, cultural and class discrimination and the mass destruction of the black family are growing dangers that threaten everyone of us. Because we have remained steadfast in this self-destructive behavior among one another, we have mitigated a prosperous future for our children. Our heritage demands that we seek a truce toward this madness. We have to return to the establishment of hierarchical roles in our homes and relationships.

Let the wives begin to give leading roles back to the husbands. I have jokingly said that Queen Ester became a queen simply because of a disobedient wife. However the husband needs to know that with leadership comes great responsibilities. Leadership is not ownership. A man does not own his wife, he owns the responsibility of being the head of his home. Her safety and security become his everlasting obligation.

What makes a woman safe? Financial stability, tranquility, love, spirituality, and family unity. A man must create a financially independent home for his wife. He must establish and work to sustain a peaceful home for his wife. He should encourage and support family unity. He must be loving to his wife. He also must have a spiritual relationship with his wife.

A wife is safe if she has a peaceful home to go to everyday. She is safe if she has a loving husband in her life. She is safe if she has a husband who has a spiritual relationship with her. But none of these things can be accomplished if the wife does not give the leadership role to the husband. It is not her responsibility to be the leader in the marriage. When she takes on the role of a leader in the marriage or relationship, she has just signed herself up for a relationship contract.

A relationship in which the woman has taken on the lead role is not a relationship, it is a contract. The same can be said of a marriage. A wife should always maintain family bonding. These are her strengths, settling family disputes, conflicts, and maintaining family closeness. Circumstances should not allow a woman to take on the role of a man in any relationship. When she meets a man, the first thing that she should look for in him is his care for her safety. Remember! A good man is a man who cares for the safety of his wife or his girlfriend.

The family is the main focus of this new deal. Most black family today exist only by blood line. Conflicts and malevolent attributions rule our homes today. Our fights against one another are carried out with very distasteful results. Sisters against sisters and brothers against brothers. The strength of the modern day black family relies on strangers, rather than kinfolks. In other words, we tend to trust total strangers with valuable assets instead of family support. Our best friends are somebody else instead of our family members.

When a family member faces a problem, we surprisingly salivate towards their trials. Today family fights last for decades passing on to another generation. The failure of most black families is the driven force behind poverty, crime and despair. A successful family is define by their willingness to settle conflicts, maintained good structure and relentlessly pursue family unity. One of the great danger of the black family today is our willingness to sustain family quarrels and established family favorites. Everyone has a favorite family member with whom they can trust.

When ever we choose a favorite family member in our family, we always tend to either isolate other members in the family or believe that we are the only sound thinkers in the family. We also indulge in plutonic relationships with our family. Dialogue among many families today consist of a somewhat forced obligation between both participants. A brief mention of a black on black crime on television, is enough for some of us. The family good names means nothing to many of us anymore.

Black families today live farther apart than past generations. Our places of worship are different, and even the friends that we keep are also different from other family members. We have become very competitive against one another. We use our children as a competitive tool against the children of other family members. Our spouses are involved in the competition. Our homes, clothes, jobs, and even our friends, they all play pivotal roles in the competition. we use every blessing as a competitive tool or a boast against one another. we denigrate family members who are less educated or financially stable. We flaunt our wealth at one another, and we sometimes avoid socializing with family members who we perceived  as less fortunate than we are.

# Chapter 11:
# Hate

There is a trickle down effect that becomes part of our family demises. Cousins, nieces and nephew and even family friends, they all see the divisiveness and they immediately take sides with their favorites. spouses and family of spouses are not fighting anymore in today family. The behavior is I stay away from you and you stay away from me. This goes on for many years. Family history is barely mention these days, unless when there is a tragedy in the family, or relatives purposely seeks to know the family history for themselves.

Our anger and animosities against one another are incomprehensible to basic logic. When we riot, we destroy our neighborhoods. Some of us drive in our neighborhoods with loud music blasting from our cars radio. But when we are in other ethnic neighborhoods, we tend to lower our music. Our community is inflicted with a wave of misguided knowledge of our elected officials. As I mentioned earlier in the book, elected public officials who make very important laws and by-laws in our community seem to become of no importance during the electoral seasons.

We are slowly pursuing jobs that are meaningful toward our community progress. Our voting practices need to be strongly evaluated by many of us. We live in the same crime infested neighborhood for many years, voting for the same political leader who promises the same change for many years. Our votes are without knowledge. Many of us appear clueless as to the importance of jobs such as county prosecutors, appeal court judge, traffic court judge, and even county coroner. All of these jobs play very major roles in the African American community. A county prosecutor is a very important individual to the black community. So is an appellate court judge. The traffic court judge is also a very important person in the African American community. All of these people have made a major difference in the lives of many African American community.

There is a growing wave of xenophobic countenance brewing amongst some of us. Our beliefs and opinions are sounding more xenophobic with no truth claimed to them.. Most African American belief that their rights and privileges as Americans have been given to foreigners from oversea. Arabs merchants and Arab students are taken a brunt of these beliefs. Many African American are becoming first in line to tell a foreigner to go back where they came from.

The following beliefs: foreign workers in the United States do not pay taxes until after five (5) years. This is not a true claim. Some even belief that working foreigners do not pay taxes regardless. Colleges and universities do not charge foreign students for tuitions. This is also not a true claim. A foreign student books and housing are all free and paid for by the United States government. Another false claim.

Robberies against Arabs merchants are frowned on by many of us in the black community, however, some questioned the presence of those merchants in the black neighborhood. The size and many tasks that we as a people face today are great, economic and social growth, better health care availability, higher education for more of our youths, active roles in our communities, youth violence, etc . for too long our focuses have been placed on our young black men striving for excellence and reaching for the stars. Some of our black men have reached for those stars and others are avoiding their plight for those stars.

Today the black community is asking for many second chances for our youth. We believe that our youth can and will succeed if giving the chance to succeed. And many of our youth have demonstrated their emotionless respond toward youth violence and family chaos. Our preaching and teaching have become bottomless songs of repetition to our youth. Fosters homes, group homes, and boot camp have become the new get away for many of our youth today. Our neighborhoods have become very desensitize to crimes. Our occasional cries of stop the violence have become destututed to the ears of our youth. Spiritual desolation have taken place in most of our lives. Our roles have change in the community. Our young have taken on the adult role and the adults have taken on the young role. Adults and juveniles are becoming partners in criminal activities. Shame is no more a deterrent.

The African American community have ran out of excuses. Africa have ran out of excuses also. Many of us have grown older and we are still seeing images of African children on television needing help. Our definition of help have change over the years. Also our definition of opportunity is slowly changing.

We had an African as the secretary general for the united nations. A leader over many nations with economic and military power, yet, the genocidal bloodshed that went on in Rwanda was not intervene immediately. The world is slowly opening up to change. Women are becoming very effective leaders around the globe. Many blacks are representing very reputable organization around the globe.

Our focus need to shift toward our young black girls immediately. Black women have always been the hidden secret in many successful black men lives. With a black woman on our side, our weaknesses are strengthen. Our intellects are show case. And our strengths are renew everyday. Many black women have raised very strong and powerful leaders today.

In the year 1660s, legal documents and colonial statute maintained manipulative laws overshadowing the birth right of a black child. Bills of sale began to stipulate that the children of black female servants would also be servants for life. In 1662 the House of Burgesses decreed that a child's condition---free or unfree---followed that of the mother. So the black man had no legal rights to his son/daughter during slavery, according to the law. Although non---existing today, the logic is still the same, attack the black woman you win the war. Young black girls are having babies. Young black girls are making very poor choices when they are choosing a mate. Young black girls are accepting physical abuses as a symbol of expressed love. Young black girls are settling for less. When we stop them, we can stop our young men.

Our understanding of community should not just be subjected only to us alone. We must include other races. No one race can win this war on family dysfunction. Race relation plays the pivotal role in a renew effort to take back our family from violence. Family values would cease to exist if we continue to ignore the family. Our values and dignity should be insisted upon our youths. Our skin color should hold no more significant in values than our character. The implementation of ideas and plans should be share with all races, in order to win the war.

We must now become part of every aspect of our society. We must become understandably involved in the political system very actively. We also have to introduce the political system and its significance to our youths.

# CHAPTER 12: NEW LEADERS & PIONEERS

We have to teach ourselves the functioning system of global and national politics. Voting for the same person for life should become something of the past.

New leaders should be sought after and encouraged. Progress should be seen not always promise to us. We should also obtain knowledge of our local governing system. Our understanding of the law should be broad and revisited often in-order to be aware of new changes. And as I revisit the importance of family once more, I strongly request that every African American and Africans to go back to our ancestral love for their family, and their community.

As was stated earlier, many slaves went back into captivity, trying to free their family and friends from slavery. Our advancement and greater achievements are yet to come. But we must realize all of our weakness, and faults and used them as a reminder to a mistake that once held us down. We must reach to that family member who has isolated him/herself from the family. Family conflicts and quarrels should not advance to anarchy in the family.

Now is the time that we must put away foolish thoughts and decisions for the true calling of our goals and ambitions in life. We must remind ourselves that the destruction of a family do not come from the outside, instead, it starts from the inside. There is no nation on earth that have falling due to outside invaders. Internal conflicts have destroyed empires. The fall of the Roman Empire was due to internal conflicts.

The following empires also experienced the same fate due to internal conflicts: The Mali, the British, the Hittites, the Assyrians, the Chaldeans, the Persians, Songhai, the Almorvids, the Sosso, and modern day Russian Empire. All of those empires fell to internal conflicts giving way to out side intervention. There have been a universal anarchy that have plaque world peace for so long, causing despondencies, and desolations in families and communities. The Tutsis and Hutsis savage battle that brought world shame to the continent of Africa showed the effects of silence. The blood diamond impetuosity in Sierra Leone shine a light on material greed.

Totalitarianism in Zimbabwe, Sudan massacre and community violence in South Africa with the carnage of civil war in Liberia, along with the Nigerian oil, anarchy all of these have implicated the real urgent need for true tranquility and respect in all of these beautiful nations.

The will to stop this madness strongly over power the will of the very few that have continued its course. However a growing number of us have allowed these individuals to instill a cloud of impuissance upon us. We must not allowed our culture, and dignity to be define by the shameful acts of the very few in our community. Speaking against crimes and violence have become prevalent in our society for too long.

Crimes and violence against each other have been spoken against since the 60s,70s80s,90, and now currently. We have become prevaricators toward confronting the issue of crimes against each other. We must spread the message of zero tolerance toward youth crimes in our community. Many of our leaders today have spoken long and tired enough. It is time for us to join in not only by singing and marching, But by taking actions such as enforcing laws in our communities, and evoking our leaders to demonstrate true dedication toward our community. This also involves each one of us speaking, snitching, and exposing our brothers and sisters who have purposely decided to continued in this path of destruction against the black community.

As we move forward in this new fight to eliminate violence against each other and strengthening our family unity, I would like us to remind ourselves of the names of the original fighters for peace among us. Samuel Cornish, Harriet Tubman, Booker T. Washington, W. E. Dubois Richard Allen, Absalom Jones, Jupiter

Hammon, Daniel Coker, John Chavis, Marcus Garvey, Black abolitionist David walker who urged black men to redeem themselves by defending their loved ones from slavery in the 1830s.Nat Turner, and countless others.

I once again share with you the names and the sacrificial labors of another group of early pioneers of democracy and equality. Lemuel Haynes the first ordained black congregationalist minister, serving as pastor to several white congregations. James Forten who volunteered to serve as a powder boy with a cannon crew on board the American Privateer Royal Louis in 1781. Forten was a deeply patriotic American who refused special treatment from the son of a British officer when Forten was taken prisoner in battle. William Wells Brown the first African American novelist, his Clotel; or the President's Daughter, published in 1853, used Thomas Jefferson and Sally Hemings affair to explore the moral ramifications of many slaveholders who fathered children with their slaves. Martin Delany, another black novelist during the antebellum years, his work, His Blake, or the Huts of America.

Our history continues: Henry Highland Garnet who was a staunched advocate for black nationalism. Henry Garnet may be seen as the Malcolm X of his generation, differentiating his views from that of Frederick Douglas who was dedicated to nonviolence. Garnet was the first African American to deliver a sermon in the United States congress. Oladah Equiano who was sold to European slave traders, he received schooling in

Europe which him to work as a shipping clerk and a amateur navigator. Equiano helped organize a colony that fought to emancipate British slaves in Sierra Leone.

Other known pioneers are: Crispus Attucks who became the first African American to have an annual holiday in his honor. Attucks was the first American to attack the British soldiers during the Boston Massacre. He became an American hero and the state of New Jersey declared March 5 as a holiday in his memory. Absalom Jones who was the first African American to petition Congress requesting that slavery be abolished. James McCune Smith, the first African American to earn a medical degree. He earned his degree from the University of Glasgow in Scotland in 1837.

Here are more pioneers and institutions; Samuel Cornish along with John Russwurm published the Freedom's Journal, the first African American newspaper in 1827. Joseph Cinque who rebelled against Spanish slave merchants aboard a ship called the Amistad, meaning friendship. Cinque resilience caused fifty-four African slaves to be free. Madison Washington who also led another revolt aboard a slave ship called the Creole. He sailed the vessel to the Bahamas where he and 135 slaves became free.

Martin Delany 1812to 1885 adamantly insisted that African Americans should control their own destiny. Martin Delany was a journalist, an anthropologist and a doctor. Miflin Gibbs the only African American to serve two nations as an elected political official.

Martin served as a councilman in Victoria British Columbia Canada, and he was also elected judge in little rock Arkansas in 1873. David Walker who lead a tireless effort to abolish slavery. James and Lucretia Mott, Charles T. Torrey who organized the underground railroad in the East than any other location. Barack H. Obama the first African American President of the United States of America.

Understanding how we arrived to this point is crucial to our salvation from this battle. The African culture is the foundation and the mother of all cultures. Replica of African arts, customs, and even civilization have been practiced by many nations and cultures throughout history. The beauty of being black is a gift from God. Our smiles, language, custom, dialects, women, children, men, arts have all been artistically projected, and adored globally as possibly a wonder. According to history, our world derived from the mother land of Africa. So many cultures, race, and ethnic group can called Africa their mother land.

Emotions and opinions are all natural phenomenon of mankind. Reading this book, one should have an honest reflection of ourselves and our communities. This book is not a condemnation of my people, it is a revelation to hidden obstacles that have kept us in bondage for centuries. Our history is world history. The Ethiopians, Ghanaians, Malians, Libyans, and other African nations in counting. The Greeks and Romans all shared a piece of black history (African History). Nevertheless, the history of Africa is one of inclusiveness. Africans accepted European, the Greeks, the Portuguese and nationals of all walks of life during the great trade migration. Our struggles should now be fought for all mankind, eliminating poverty, diseases, economic deprivations, crimes against one another locally and globally.

I would like to thank my wife for her support and help in making this dream come true. To my three beautiful children Cierra Lynne, Peter Allen and Zachary Peter Oduwole. Daddy loves you all and remember to always strive for results. Results are better than debates.

To my parents, thank you for raising me as a Christian and a descent person. I did just what you expected of all of your children.

To all of my brothers and sisters thank you for all of your support. My Childhood memories and experiences with all of you have helped me in so many ways.

To all of my nephews, cousins, nieces and host of family members, you all are part of this...........

To all of my friends, please buy my book!!!!!!!!! I truly love each and everyone of you. I know that you guys are in my corner.

To my in-laws thank you for giving me Freda. I love you guys. To my church family, thank you for all of your prayers and support.

To my Lord and Savior Jesus Christ, I thank you for your protection, your loving kindness and your mercy.

For many years I have always wondered the root behind the many pitfalls of the black community. Why are we still fighting battles once fought by our forefathers? Why are we easily ruled by few people? Why African countries with a 95% black population are easily ruled by only a 5% white minority? Why has black on black violence lasted for so long in our communities? Why do we become angry when one of us asks these questions? With many years of praying and soul searching, I believe that I have found the answer to these questions.

The disunity of the black family, starting from Africa to the Americas, is the root to this plague. My mother has a saying, "if your family do not sell you, the streets will not buy you". The story of Joseph in the bible always comes to mind when ever she makes that quote. Because we have been fighting among ourselves for so long we have given others the strength to rule us. This book is an education for me and you!

A Brief History & Some Thoughts

I am just an ordinary Christian who loves to explore, read, and seek positive results in life.

As a young kid, I always knew that I wanted to be a narrator. Ironically, shyness became a hidden secret to my dream.

My favorite books in the bible are the books of the old testament. I am a junkie when it comes to world history. I became interested with current events, world history, and politics at the early age of fourteen. By age fifteen, I had read every book of the encyclopedia.

King David is my favorite biblical leader. But it was the story of Joseph that inspired in me the need to put family first.

I believe that the ideas and opinions of most people are derived from a single person in life.

Although I took my children to the zoo, I have always frowned on animals in captivity.

I believe that the strength to any community is the unity of the family.

The strength of a united family overpowers the evil plan of their enemies.

In a marriage, 50% contribution should not be a demanded requirement by each spouse.

Spousal contribution in a marriage varies on a day to day basis.

Most marriages and relationships are sustained by the extra efforts of one spouse. One person usually covers the many loose ends of a marriage or a relationship in order to sustain that marriage or relationship.

Most women believe that they do more in a relationship than their partner.

I believe words are very powerful tools used today to persuade people.

There are many among us who would trade anything to obtain power.

The three most powerful people in a society are: a police officer, a judge, and the news media.

I believe twenty should be the legal age.

I believe very strong punishment deters crimes.

I never understood how plea deals work in court. Get caught doing a crime and you are allowed to tell the judge you are not guilty.

I believe that most people would rather see themselves better than their peers. Most people are more jealous than they believe.

I believe a woman chooses her mate, not the man as we think.

I believe sex is the weakness of all men.

I believe women are more quick to trust  people than men are.

A woman is vulnerable to hurt because of her will to trust.

I believe women handle stress better than men do.

# BIBLIOGRAPHY

Hine, Darlene Clark. THE AFRICAN - AMERI-
CAN ODYSSEY. William C. Hine, Stanley Harrold.
Upper Saddle River, New Jersey: Prentice Hall, 2000.